Amazon Echo Look

The Comprehensive Guide

Chris James

Table of Contents

Introduction

Amazon Echo Look is a fascinating device that comprises of Amazon's latest addition to their Echo-branded devices. It is the fourth device, aside from the original Echo, Amazon Tap, and the Echo Dot.

The Amazon Echo Look is primarily a camera that can enable you to snap pictures and take videos at any time you desire. It does feature a speaker that enables you to hear Alexa as she speaks, as well as a unique service that enables you to capture each of your daily outfits, catalogue them, and receive real-time style advice.

This device is a state of the art creation that has fascinating features that make it a major advantage to anyone who purchases it. If you are interested in learning more about this incredible device and how you can use it to your advantage, then you have come to the right place. "*Amazon Echo Look: The Comprehensive Guide*" is designed to help you get all of the insider's information on how this amazing device works and what you can use it for.

Technology is rapidly advancing, and it is important to stay ahead of the curve. Learning the ins and outs of new devices can enable you to understand where technology is advancing to, and how you can use it to enhance your life. This comprehensive guide will discuss every aspect of your life that can be enhanced and benefited by the Amazon Echo Look, and how you can start using yours today. If you are prepared to change your life with this cutting edge technology, then dive in! Each chapter has been created to help you master a unique feature of your new device, so take your time and allow yourself to get acquainted with your new Echo Look. And of course, enjoy!

Chapter 1: Getting Started

The Amazon Echo Look itself is unlike any of the Echo-branded creations that came before it. Unlike those devices which emphasized the quality of your audio experience with music playback, the Echo Look is all about camera features. It has a high-quality camera attached to it which has the ability to allow you to snap photographs and shoot videos at any time you desire. It also features an incredible program that allows you to catalogue your daily outfits so that you can receive real-time style advice each day.

Ultimately, Amazon Echo Look is said to feature everything that people ever loved about their Alexa-enhanced devices, except now she can assist you with looking your best on a daily basis.

How Does It Work?

You can mount your Amazon Echo Look onto a wall using the mounting kit, or you can sit it on your dresser. Once it is placed, you can activate it using voice commands. The Echo Look can take full-length photos, as well as short videos of you. The camera has a depth-sensing feature, as well as LED lights for flash, and computer vision that enables the camera to blur the background out of your shots.

The primary idea behind Amazon Echo Look is that you can use it to see yourself from all angles. Through taking photographs, you can build a personal look book of all of your outfits, and either share them with others or get advice from "fashion specialists" based on the Echo Look algorithms.

In addition to this incredible new style advice service, the Echo Look still enables you to tap into Alexa so that you can get all of the information that you would with any other Echo device, including weather updates, controlling smart home devices, and more.

What Do You Get with It?

If you are waiting for your Echo Look device to arrive, or if you haven't opened the box yet, then you might be wondering what's inside. The Amazon Echo Look comes with the device itself, as well as a screw-on base and a standard tripod socket. You also get a 21W power adapter that has an 8-foot cord, and a wall-mounting kit that enables you to hang it anywhere you desire. The Amazon Echo Look can be placed anywhere, so long as the power adapter can reach a wall socket.

What Is Inside of the Echo Look to Make It Work?

If you were to look inside of the Amazon Echo Look, you would discover several sensors and technology enhancements that make this device work the way it does. It includes the voice-activated Alexa machine, dual-band, dual-antenna, Wi-Fi connectivity, a 5-megapixel camera, front lighting, a flash, a microphone, a speaker, and a mic/camera off button as well as an indicator.

Based on the way the device is built, you can access cloud-based media storage options, however, you cannot access AUX audio input/output or Bluetooth audio input/output with Alexa. You also can't use this device with the Alexa Voice Remote. However, you can use the Alexa app, as well as a companion app that has been designed which is called Echo Look.

Setting Up Your Device

Every Echo device enables you to set it up so you can use the Alexa features, and Echo Look is no different. You can use the Alexa mobile app or web app with this device, which can provide you with access to tips on how to use Alexa better. You will want to set up Alexa first before you set up the rest of your device. When you're done, set up the Echo Look app as well, so that you can get a full range of use out of your device.

After completing the set up for Alexa, as well as the Echo Look app, you can start setting up your Echo Look device. This part is simple. You want to plug in the device, and place it or mount it somewhere where you will be able to stand back and give the camera the ability to see your full-body. From there, you want to turn it on and then use your voice to start commanding the device. You might say, for example, "Alexa, take a video" and then turn around so that the device can capture a full 360 view of the outfit you are wearing.

Alexa

As with the other Echo-branded devices, Alexa is present in the Echo Look. She works the exact same as the Alexa in other devices, as well. You can use Alexa to read the news or audiobooks, set alarms, to control your smart home devices, get weather and traffic updates, check your commute, order from Starbucks or other restaurants, access your digital calendars, and more. If you are unsure about what you can do using Alexa, simply say the command "Alexa, tell me what I can do" and she will go into detail about the many options she has to offer.

Why the Echo Look?

Many people may be wondering why Amazon created Echo Look in the first place. What is the benefit of having the built-in

Style Check? At first, the answer was unclear. People were unsure as to what the overall benefit of this was, especially considering that Amazon is not offering the opportunity to purchase any new clothes along with the Echo Look. So, what benefit are they getting?

For now, Amazon will be tracking photographs with the outfit compare options. Whenever you submit your photographs to Style Check, real-life fashion experts will be answering to decide which one they prefer and what you should wear. The belief is that they will be tracking the overall data of what people are wearing and where style is going. Then, in the future, they can use this data to provide you with specific information for what you can purchase for your wardrobe, and they will be able to stay up to date with overall national and international clothing trends.

At this time, people prefer to purchase clothes in-store. Being able to see and try on the clothes is best because you can get an idea of how it fits, what the style is like, and if it suits you or not. However, imagine if Amazon knew all of this intimate information about you and your preferences. Then, they would be able to provide you with clothing options that met these exact specifics. You would be able to shop through Alexa without ever having to leave your house to go through the process of digging through clothing racks and trying on clothes. Instead, they would be chosen and sent to you. It opens up a world of potential for online retailers in the clothing and accessory industry.

In addition to using your own data to serve you, in particular, this type of data gives Amazon the opportunity to have leverage in the fashion industry. They could use their analysis to create unique and exclusive partnerships with fashion companies so that they can start producing their own clothing lines and offer custom sizing options as well as their infamous next-day shipping services.

Echo Look Style Check

To use this feature, you first ask Alexa to take a photograph or video of you. Do this with two outfits. Then, you will want to open your Echo Look app. From there you have the option to blur the background and share the image with your friends. You also get the option to add it into your own look book. In addition to those three options, you can use the Style Check feature that will allow you to submit two of the photographs for a second opinion to figure out which style looks better. The decision will be based on fit, color, current trends, and styling. The more you use this feature and feedback and input is given, the better this feature will work.

Ultimately, the Amazon Echo Look is a fascinating revolution for the Echo devices. It appears as though Amazon is seeking to use the Echo devices, completed with Alexa, to leverage their ability to serve you in every possible way in your life. Now you have a voice-command enabled device that will tell you anything you need to know for personal management, as well as one that will help you decide what to wear and eventually even help you purchase new clothes. It is a fascinating futuristic device that is certainly worth learning about.

Chapter 2: Voice Controlling Smart Home Appliances

If you are new to the world of Amazon Echo, then you are probably curious about all of the many incredible features that come along with this product line. The Echo Look features all of the same great advantages of its older siblings, including the ability to use voice-commands on smart home appliances.

The future of the world lies in voice-command technology, not unlike what Alexa offers to your home. When outfitted with the right devices, your entire home can be controlled through Alexa, including the locks on your doors, your lights, and even your thermostat. Learning to control these devices is not difficult, and having this ability can completely change the way you live your life. Once you become used to Alexa's ability to help you control all of the functions within your house, it will almost seem like an archaic event to actually get up and do any of it on your own.

There are several features within' your home that can be controlled using Alexa, and you are about to learn about each one of them. By combining each of these unique features, you give yourself the ability to completely control your entire house and the way it functions all through your voice, or your Alexa smartphone app. It is an incredible futuristic opportunity to have an entire home that contains technology that we once only dreamed of. The future is now, and Alexa is a major part of that.

Smart Hubs

Smart hubs are, essentially, centers for the automated devices within' your home to connect to so that you can control them with Alexa. When you have multiple smart devices in your home, you will want to use a hub which will allow their signals to be organized so that they can be voice-controlled and controlled through your Alexa mobile app and web app effortlessly. These are essential tools for every automated home that uses Alexa to operate regular functions. There are several brands of smart hubs available, simply pick the best one within' your budget that operates well with Amazon Echo and Alexa so that you can use it to organize and operate your smart home.

Smart Bulbs

Smart bulbs are LED bulbs that you plug into standard lightbulbs sockets so that you can gain all of the benefits of smart technology. You can turn the bulbs on or off, and with many types of bulbs, you can even choose which color they will shine. As with most smart technology, there are various brands available. Simply pick the one that serves the need that you have. Smart lightbulbs can be used with lamps, built-in lighting in your ceiling, and anywhere else that a regular lightbulb fits. There are various sizes and shapes, so simply pick the one that suits your needs.

Smart Dimmers and Switches

For further customizability with your smart lighting system, you can get smart dimmers and switches. Again, these allow you to turn lights on or off. If you have a smart dimmer, you can also control the brightness of the bulb using Alexa voice-commands, or your mobile app.

Smart Outlets

To control non-smart technology, you can use smart outlets. These outlets are plugged into your standard outlet sockets and used to control anything plugged into them using the smart voice system. They can be turned on or off, and even put on a schedule so that they operate only when you want them to. Not all smart outlet devices are compatible with Alexa, so make sure that you choose the right brand that will work with your device.

Smart Door Locks

Now, you can install special door locks onto your door so that you can control those using Alexa voice-commands. These locks are used in conjunction with smart home hubs, and allow you to lock your door effortlessly either using your voice or your app. For security reasons, you cannot unlock your door using this application or voice-command system, however. There are many companies that are compatible with Alexa and various smart hubs, so simply shop around and find the best system for your household.

Smart Alarm Systems

Smart alarm systems allow you to arm your house no matter where you are. They operate extremely similar to smart door locks. For the same reason as the door locks, you cannot unarm your house using the Alexa system, so make sure that you are prepared to unarm it on your own when you arrive home. Again, there are many brands to choose from, so simply pick the one that works best for your family.

Smart Thermostats

Although it may sound extremely difficult, smart thermostats actually fit in directly where your existing thermostat is. There is no need to alter the wiring system or use any fancy installation methods. Simply plug it in where your existing thermostat is and connect it to Wi-Fi. Then, you will be able to control the temperature of your home using Alexa. Note, if you don't want to connect the thermostat to your Wi-Fi, you can connect it to your smart hub as well.

Smart Garage Doors

Smart garage door openers allow you to close your garage door using Alexa technology. Just like with locks and alarm systems, however, you cannot open your door using Alexa for security purposes.

Smart Gadgets

You can use specific smart hubs that are designed to work with entertainment systems and devices to control your gadgets in your home. These devices can be used to turn things such as your TV on and off, as well as control other features such as volume and channels. You can use these hubs with various gadgets and devices, depending on what the hub is compatible with.

Smart Appliances

There are a variety of smart appliances available now which enable you to use Alexa for various tasks. For example, smart fridges can now be used to add something to your shopping list, or even place grocery orders for you. You don't even have to tap on your fridge like a giant tablet, you can simply do it through voice-command. You can also use smart washers and dryers to start loads and see how much time is left. Of course, they have developed smart ovens as well. You can use Alexa to preheat your oven or turn it off. You can also turn on air conditioners and water heaters using their smart appliance technology. There are a variety of different smart appliances available on the market, depending on what you are searching for. Almost every time of appliance has been turned into a smart appliance now.

Smart Ceiling Fans

If you still use ceiling fans in your home, you can use Alexa to turn them on and off now. There are a variety of ceiling fans that are available that enable you to control their speed as well as the lights attached to them using Alexa technology.

Your entire home can be automated using Alexa technology. At this time, they are even designing features inside of cars that will be able to be activated and controlled using Alexa. Soon, your entire day-to-day life will be able to be enhanced using this technology. Systems that you once had to spend time on and think about will now be automated or completed using simple voice-commands, and you will be able to invest your time elsewhere. For example, you can enjoy your smart house, spend more time with loved ones, and pay attention to expanding your career and business. Without having to invest so much time on the day-to-day workings of your home and life, you will be able to enjoy other things instead.

Chapter 3: Arranging Purchases

One of the incredible things about Echo products is that you can use them to purchase items using your voice. Alexa, the voice-command program, allows you to use your voice to purchase any item you desire. Being able to use this feature means that you can effortlessly buy anything you need, which can make shopping incredibly easy. You no longer need to search for products, pull out your card, or put any effort into shopping. You simply ask, and you receive.

History of Alexa Purchases

When Echo was originally released, you could only purchase items that you had previously purchased on Amazon. There was also a handful of specially selected products that could be purchased using your voice, regardless of whether you had purchased them before or not. Now, the selected product line has expanded to include nearly everything from the Amazon website, making online shopping a whole lot easier.

Purchasing Abilities and Limitations

Although you can now purchase more than ever using Alexa's help, there are still some limitations towards what you can and cannot purchase. The purchasing ability rule is simple: nearly everything available on Amazon Prime is available to be purchased through Alexa. The limitations are a little grander than that, however. Using Alexa, you cannot purchase the following things: shoes, apparel, jewelry, Amazon Fresh items, watches, Amazon Prime Now items, Amazon Prime Pantry items, and Add-On items. All of these are not eligible to be purchased through Alexa, yet. Although, it is expected that these will be added to the lineup in the near future.

How to Purchase Using Alexa

If you want to make convenient purchases using your Alexa-enabled Echo device, there are a few things you need to set up first. Once you do, you can start using your device to purchase almost anything you want.

First, you are going to need to log in to your Alexa app and turn on voice purchasing. If this feature is not on, you will not be able to make purchases through Alexa at all. If it is on, you will be able to start using Alexa for making purchases at your own desire.

A good idea when you are setting up Alexa purchases is to set up the four-digit PIN code through Alexa. This means that anytime you are going to use your Echo device to purchase something, you will have to provide the PIN. Without it, no purchases can be made. This prevents people from making purchases on your device, which creates a greater sense of security around the voice-command purchasing options.

Before you start making any purchases with Alexa, make sure you check your 1-click shipping settings. You will want to make sure that your payment options and shipping address are correct before you start making any purchases using Alexa.

Once you are ready to make your purchases, simply turn on your Echo Look device and begin using your voice to make your purchases! All you have to say is "Alexa, order (product name)", and Alexa will place the order using your 1-click settings. If you are unsure of the exact product you want to order, use a more generic phrase like "Alexa, order cat food". Alexa will then give you the top search results for what you are looking for. If they are not what you are looking for, say "No" and Alexa will give you the next result. You can do this until Alexa reads off the proper item and then you can ask Alexa to order it. When you have identified the correct item, you can provide Alexa with your 4-digit PIN and Alexa will order it for you. It's that simple!

After you have placed your order for the item through Alexa, you will find the order confirmation details in your Alexa app. This will be your receipt for the order you have placed.

The Importance of the 4-Digit PIN

It is extremely important that you put together a 4-digit PIN for Alexa. If not, purchases can be made without your discretion, and they can be charged to your card. In some cases, Alexa has been reported to order tons of items without the owner actually prompting her to. Recently, a TV news reporter was reporting on Alexa and prompted several people's Echo devices to order several dollhouses as a result of the report.

Making purchases through Amazon has never been easier. With the help of Alexa, you can order almost anything from the Amazon website using your voice. It is extremely simple to set up your Alexa features and use them at your own will. Always make sure that you set up your 4-digit PIN, however, to prevent your device from making any orders that you did not intend for. This will protect you from fraudulent or accidental orders. It's that simple!

Chapter 4: IFTTT Guide

If you are new to Echo and Alexa, then you are likely unfamiliar with IFTTT. IFTTT stands for "If This Then That", which gives you the option to program your Echo to perform certain functions for you automatically. For example, you can have it set to *if* (news network) uploads a new story *then* send yourself said story by email. There are many different types of IFTTT settings you can toy with, so long as you have the time to play around with it and learn more. This guide will help you figure out exactly how you can set up new IFTTT settings.

Getting Started with IFTTT

The first thing you must do is create an IFTTT account. You can do this simply by going to the IFTTT website and creating your own account using the credentials that they request from you for the process. Once you have, you can get started with connecting your IFTTT account to Alexa so that you can start triggering various situations automatically.

To connect the two, you want to go onto your Alexa channel page and click "Connect". This button will allow you to connect your IFTTT account to your Alexa account. You do this by sharing some of your Amazon account information with your IFTTT account. Once you're done inputting the required information you can click "Okay" and you will be directed back to IFTTT.

The next step will be to go to the iOS Reminders channel and click "Connect". From there, you will download and install the

20

IFTTT for iOS program (called IF on iOS) and then connect the channel with the walk-through instructions provided by the app. Once you are done, you can click "Done".

This marks the completion of the setup process. After you have completed these three simple steps, you can begin creating your IFTTT triggers so that you can actively use all of the benefits provided by this unique feature for your Echo Look device.

Creating IFTTT Triggers

The first step to getting your IFTTT triggers set up is to open the IFTTT application and click "this". In there, you will find a channel called "Amazon Alexa", which you will want to click. Once you have clicked the Amazon Alexa channel, you can begin looking through the various triggers available to you. When you've found one, simply click "Create Trigger". This will complete the first step of the process.

Next, you want to go to the "that" list, and scroll until you find the result that you want the trigger to cause. When you have decided on the result and set it in place, you will be guided through a process that will enable you to put that result in action. Following that, you will be able to complete the process of setting up your result.

Lastly, you want to click "Create Action", and then finish the entire process by clicking "Create Recipe". This entire process is going to allow you to create various IFTTT actions. You can create as many as you want for as many different purposes as you desire. Ideally, you should keep your Alexa-driven tasks under a custom list named "Alexa" so you can easily discover what you are looking for.

Creating IFTTT "recipes" allows you to customize your Alexa. You can use this as an opportunity to complete virtually anything you desire with your Echo Look. These triggers and results can be set up for a number of different actions, so take your time and browse through. Soon enough, your Alexa will be completely capable of helping you with every action you need assistance with in your life.

Chapter 5: Echo Look as an Assistant

Amazon Echo Look together with Alexa technology makes for the perfect digital assistant for anyone. With Echo Look's new technology, the device is even greater of an assistant now than it ever was before. And, as we can project, it is only getting better from here.

Personal assistants are intended to assist with important tasks that take up a great amount of time in your life: shopping, helping you pick your wardrobe, managing the smaller things such as household functions. With Echo Look's technology, you can now do this with your Alexa-enabled device as well.

Purchasing

As you learned previously, your Echo device makes for an excellent tool when you are looking to purchase new things. It can help you with ordering groceries, animal food, and many other things. When you are busy, it can make shopping extremely simple. While you are completing other tasks in your life, you can simply ask Alexa to do your shopping for you and it will be completed. Once you are done shopping, everything you have ordered will be shipped directly to your door.

Being able to shop in this new-age convenient manner means that you no longer have to waste time shopping in stores. You do not have to search aisles for what you are looking for, wait in long lineups, or even deal with the traffic and process of driving to the shop itself. Everything is simple and automated using Alexa technology, which makes it extremely easy and uses significantly less time on your behalf.

Wardrobe

As you have learned with the new Echo Look device, you can now use the Style Check and Look Book options as an opportunity to get assistance with your wardrobe. You can get personalized fashion advice, find out what looks good and what doesn't, and learn exactly what type of items fit your unique build the best. That way, when you do go shopping for clothes, you know exactly what to look for. Also, since you can have an on-demand look book of your current wardrobe, you can easily see how new clothes and accessories will fit in with what you already have.

The future of Alexa and the Echo Look Style Check technology is also promising, likely enabling you to purchase form-fitting clothes online with Alexa in no time. Overall, it makes clothes shopping and dressing significantly easier. You can find out exactly what looks great on you and what doesn't suit you quite as well. You will never be left questioning outfits again.

Managing Day-to-Day Life

Alexa technology has many valuable features that are present on all Echo devices, including the Echo Look device. You can use Alexa to play music, turn the volume up or down, and mute or unmute music. You can ask her to play specific artists or songs, or even genres. There are several other audio-related functions she can perform as well. While the Echo Look is not focused on the audio aspect, it is still present.

In addition to music and audio tracks, you can use Alexa to help you track your time by setting alarms and timers. You can also find out what date it is, or schedule things into your calendar without ever having to open up your calendar application. You can set shopping lists, to-do lists, and other lists. You can find out what the latest news is, how the weather projections are, and what traffic is like. Alexa can help you discover what movies are playing nearby, book reservations for meals, and find other entertainment for you to enjoy. She can answer questions, such as telling you who is playing in what movies and what is most popular from particular artists or actresses/actors. She can help you perform math equations, get definitions of words, and learn to spell words. Alexa can help with updating you on sports knowledge. And, of course, Alexa can help you with purchasing things from Amazon. You can also order Uber or Lyft rides, as well as other Alexa-compatible opportunities. Alexa also allows you to control everything in your home that operates on smart technology, such as smart hubs, smart light bulbs, smart locks, and more.

Overall, Alexa has the ability to help with a grand number of things in your day-to-day life. She can provide you with information and assistance that you would normally pay a personal assistant to provide you with. As long as you have the speaker nearby, you can ask Alexa to do virtually anything for you when it comes to planning, learning important information, and figuring things out. The technology is highly futuristic and makes it extremely easy for you to use, making it effortless for you to have a digital personal assistant by your side at any given time.

Household Functions

As you have already learned, Alexa is wonderful at helping with performing household functions. When you have smart-enabled devices, you can use Alexa to take care of your home for you. She can make sure everything stays functional during the day when you are at work, or even keep everything functioning correctly when you are away on vacation. Using Alexa technology, you can make sure that your house is locked and armed, lights are being turned on and off when you desire them to be, and the temperature stays at a comfortable level. You can control when groceries are ordered and how, as well as what. There is almost nothing that you can't do using Alexa and smart-technology within' your home. The opportunities are limitless. Using Alexa, you can almost run the entire technological part of your home without any extra assistance, from anywhere.

Alexa makes for an incredible personal assistant. She can help you achieve many different tasks, and her abilities are rapidly broadening. With Amazon Echo Look, a new technology has been introduced that now allows Echo Look to assist you with managing your wardrobe and ensuring that you always look your sharpest. In addition to these latest add-ons, Alexa is still able to perform all of the exceptional functions she has ever performed in the past. With each new upgrade to Echo devices, Alexa is becoming more and more powerful, making her an incredible option for having a digital personal assistant by your side at all times.

Chapter 6: Skills, Tips and Tricks

Technology always brings about a great amount of incredible functions. Echo Look and Alexa are no different. With your new Echo Look device, there are many functions available to you that you will want to master. After all, having the ultimate voice-command digital personal assistant is significantly enhanced when you know exactly how to use it to the best of your abilities.

Learning to use your Echo Look device to its fullest function means that you can gain the opportunity to have the best digital personal assistant available to you. You learn how to gain access to all of the wonderful functions, and you can use the advantages of every single one of them to further convenience you and your life. If you want this kind of value added to your life from your digital Echo device, then the following skills, tips and tricks are exactly what you need.

Teach Alexa to Recognize Your Voice Better

Unlike in the past where you had to repeat yourself over and over into a low-quality microphone that never ended up understanding what you were saying, the Echo Look is equipped with a high-quality microphone that is constantly listening for you to say "Alexa" in your daily conversation so that she can start working for you. While this may be weird at first, you will eventually get used to it once you realize how beneficial it is to have in your life.

You want to make sure that Alexa can really get an understanding of the way you speak, so that she can successfully identify when you are talking to her. You can do this by heading into the settings on your Alexa App and clicking the "voice training" option. This allows you to work through a series of 25 different phrases that you will say out loud. You can pause the training at any time if you need to. By doing this, however, you will teach Alexa to understand your voice and your mannerisms so that she can successfully identify when you are speaking to her and when you are not. This makes your life significantly easier.

Echo Records Your Voice, Which Can Be Played On the App

One of the reasons why so many people find Alexa to be slightly disturbing at first is because she is literally always listening to the room. In addition, she records any requests that have been made to her, which can be heard on the Alexa app. If you have company over who does not want to be heard or who finds it too uncomfortable, you can always use the mute button on the device to shut the microphone off. Just remember to turn it back on when you are ready to begin using Alexa again.

Delete Recordings If You Want

In addition to recording your commands and requests, Alexa also offers you the ability to manage the recordings. If you want to, you can delete them so that you no longer have them lingering in your application. To do this, simply open the Alexa app and view the history on the app's main screen. From there, you can go to the request "cards" and delete the ones you don't want anymore. Each card will have a "more" button, which will have a "remove card" option if you click on it. You can also delete the entire recording history by going into the "Manage Your Content and Devices" setting and clicking "Your Devices", then select your Echo Device. From there, you can click "Manage Voice Recordings" and then "Delete". All of your voice recording files will be deleted and you will no longer have them available for viewing.

The Most Useful Commands

Alexa features tens, if not hundreds of unique commands that you can use to control your Echo Look device. Of course, you are not going to need to or want to use these commands on a daily basis, so knowing what the most useful and important controls are can help you narrow it down and master your Echo Look device quickly. The following list features all of the most useful Alexa commands that you should begin learning immediately. You can also use this page as a reference for when you are using your Alexa, until you become acquainted with her and can remember them on your own.

Disabling Functions

- "Alexa, stop"
- "Alexa, cancel"
- "Alexa, help"

Volume Control

- "Alexa, turn it down"
- "Alexa, softer"
- "Alexa, turn it up"
- "Alexa, louder"
- "Alexa, volume 2" (you can choose between 0-10)

Music Control

- "Alexa, play some (genre/artist of choice)"
- "Alexa, set a sleep timer for [x] minutes"
- "Alexa, pause"
- "Alexa, resume"
- "Alexa, next song"
- "Alexa, loop"
- "Alexa, restart"
- If you're listening to Pandora or iHeartRadio, you can also say:
- "Alexa, I like this song"
- "Alexa, thumbs down"

Time

- "Alexa, what time is it?"
- "Alexa, wake me up at 7am"
- "Alexa, set a timer for 15 minutes"

Weather

- "Alexa, what's the weather like in (city, state)?"

You will likely become acquainted with many more controls and functions in your time with Alexa and your Echo Look device, but these are the basics. Once you learn these functions, you will find it easy to learn and explore others. There are many positive functions available for Alexa, which you can use on your device. Look to Chapter 8 for a complete list.

Hands-Free Cooking Tool

Alexa makes for a wonderful cooking companion for anyone who likes to spend time in the kitchen. You do not need to use your hands to make her function, so you do not have to worry about frequently washing and drying your hands in fear of cross-contaminating your device with potentially harmful bacteria. Instead of having to repeatedly do this to access information from your device, you can simply ask Alexa to do it for you. You can do this by using commands like the following:

- "Alexa, set a timer for 15 minutes"
- "Alexa, how much time is left on my timer?"
- "Alexa, how many (measure) are in a (measure)?" (for conversions)
- "Alexa, add milk to my shopping list"

News Briefing

Scrolling your newsfeeds is a thing of the past. With Alexa, you can ask her to read you the news while you are performing other important tasks during the day. You will want to customize this setting before you use it, but once you do it becomes a wonderful tool that can allow you to stay up-to-date on worldly events without having to worry about losing yourself in the black hole of internet scrolling.

To customize Alexa's news briefing options, first go into your Alexa app. Then, go into "Settings" and then "Account". From there, select "Flash Briefing" and then decide what type of hourly briefings you desire to hear about. There are many different news companies that you can select from in this option, as well as unique headline types. Simply choose what you want to know about and input it into your options.

Once you have completed the customization option, you are ready to hear news briefings whenever you desire. To access them, simply say "Alexa, read me the news" or "Alexa, what's new?" and she will begin the briefing process. You should note now, however, that not all news stations have audio programs, so you will often come across the robotic tone for most of your briefing sessions. Still, it is an excellent way to hear what is going on without having to actually access your device and spend time reading it. Instead, you can listen while you are cooking, cleaning, or performing other tasks that allow you to listen and accomplish the task at the same time.

Listening to Radio, Podcasts, or Discover Weekly Playlists on Spotify

When you are interested in listening to audio recordings with your device, you can access radio stations, podcasts, and even discover weekly playlists on Spotify. To do so, simply use the following commands:

- "Alexa, play NPR" which will then cause Alexa to play your local NPR station. You can also ask for call letters such as "Alexa, play KQED"

- "Alexa, play (radio station, i.e., 94.9 FM) on TuneIn"
- "Alexa, play Fox Sports Radio on iHeartRadio"
- "Alexa, play (your choice of genre) station on Pandora"
- "Alexa, play Serial podcast on TuneIn"
- "Alexa, play my Discover Weekly playlist on Spotify"

You can use Alexa to control a variety of different audio recording programs, which you can find out more about on your Alexa app. These audio recording programs will give you the opportunity to listen to playlists that you have made or that others have made, podcasts, audio books, radio stations, and more. Simply ask Alexa to begin playing your desired audio track on your desired application and she will begin! You can then use the volume controls you learned previously to customize the experience to make it more enjoyable.

To-Do List Manager

One of the handiest functions that Alexa is useful for is her ability to manage your to-do lists. She can manage actual to-do lists, such as reminding you to pick up dry cleaning, or she can help you manage shopping lists such as by adding various products to your list. You can do so using the following commands:

- "Alexa, add (product) to my shopping list"
- "Alexa, add (task) to my to-do list"
- "Alexa, what's on my shopping list?"
- "Alexa, what's on my to-do list?"

Add Google Calendar so Alexa Can Help Plan Your Day

Google Calendars work great with Alexa, and when you synchronize yours to her she can help you plan and organize your day. Each time you want to add something to your calendar, you can do so using Alexa voice commands. You can also ask her what you are doing on set days, and she will tell you what your schedule looks like. This can make scheduling appointments and events extremely easy, and keeps you completely organized in the process. You no longer have to remember what you are doing and when, or take out your device or calendar to write it in and make sure that you get the alarm. Instead, Alexa will take care of all of that for you.

To synchronize your Google Calendar with your Echo device, go to the Alexa app and click "Settings". Then, go to "Account" and then "Calendar". From there, you can link your Google account. Once you have, you can start using the following commands to control Alexa's interactions with your calendar:

- "Alexa, what's on my calendar this weekend?"
- "Alexa, what's on my calendar on Friday?"
- "Alexa, when is my next event?"
- "Alexa, add (event) to my calendar on (date) at (time)"

Add Work and Home Address so Alexa Can Tell You About Your Daily Commute

Adding your work and home addresses to your Echo Look device can allow for Alexa to tell you information about your daily commute. She can tell you about what route to take and what traffic will be like along the route so that you know how much time to give yourself, making sure that you're always on time.

To enter your addresses into the device, go to your Alexa app and under the Settings section click "Account". Then, open "Traffic" and add your home and work addresses. Now, you can access the information by using the following commands:

- "Alexa, how is traffic?"
- "Alexa, what's my commute?"

Find Information About Local Businesses and Restaurants

Alexa has the ability to tap into Yelp so that you can find the best businesses and restaurants for you to visit. This makes it easy to find nearby restaurants to enjoy and businesses where you can fulfill your shopping needs. Because Alexa taps into Yelp, she can give you advice on virtually every store within' your town, as long as it has been uploaded on Yelp.

Before you start using Alexa for this, you need to configure your location settings on your device. Do this by going into the "Settings" section of your Alexa app and clicking "Alexa Devices", then you can select the name of your Echo Look device. From there, you can go to the "Device Location" section and enter your address. Once you have done that, you can start using Alexa to help you decide where you can shop or eat next. To do this, use the following commands:

- "Alexa, what (food or ethnicity) restaurants are nearby?"
- "Alexa, find the phone number for (name of business)"
- "Alexa, find the hours for a nearby grocery store"

Online Alexa "App"

Although you likely won't need to use this technique often, if you ever need to access the Alexa app from something other than your device, you can do so from any device that has access to the internet. Simply visit alexa.amazon.com and you will be directed to a website version of the Alexa app. From there, you can log into your Alexa account and complete all of the same functions that you could from within' the app itself.

Money-Saving Tricks and Hacks for an Echo-Friendly Smart Home

One of the best parts of having an Echo device and the Alexa technology at your disposal is being able to have a smart home system that enables you to manage your entire home from your Alexa-enabled device. There are several options you can consider when you are looking to turn your home into a smart home without having to drop a ton of money to accomplish this.

You can actually experience the magic of having your entire home voice-controlled for under $50, if you are looking to do it frugally. All you need to do is purchase smart plugs. These plugs allow you to control your devices from the Alexa app based on any parameters you have set into place. You can purchase smart plugs for under $50 each, and plug them into as many plugs in your house as you desire. Once you have, you can plug in any appliances or devices you want into each smart plug and then use your Alexa-enabled device to control them.

Setting up the devices attached to the plugs is simple: go into your Alexa device, access the Smart Home section, and follow the prompts to set up your devices in your desired fashion.

There are many benefits that you can gain from having your home set up to be a smart home. For example, you can group multiple devices together so that they are all controlled by the same parameters on Alexa. This can be beneficial for things like lights, or electronics which you would want to turn on and off all at the same times. You can also set the groups up to be room-specific so that you can say something like "Alexa, turn on the living room" and all of your living room devices will power up and be ready for you to use them, including your lights, your fan, your speaker system, and any other electronics you have connected to the device.

There are other devices you can use that are name-brand and significantly more expensive, but overall you can achieve the same goals using less expensive alternatives. This can allow you to completely transform your home into a Smart Home without having to spend hundreds of dollars to do so.

Control Spotify on Echo from Computer or Phone

If you like to use Spotify on your Echo device, you can access and control it from your computer or phone, instead of by voice if you want to. You can do this by connecting your Spotify account to the Alexa app, which can be found under "Music & Books" on the menu. Once you have done that, you can start asking various questions through voice-commands, such as:

- "Alexa, play my Discover Weekly playlist on Spotify"
- "Alexa, play Spotify" (starts playing where you left off previously)
- "Alexa, play country music on Spotify"

Or, you can start controlling the Echo from your Spotify desktop and mobile apps. From this section, you can adjust the

Echo's volume, queue, and songs. You can also play, pause, or skip the songs remotely when the app says "You are listening on (name of Echo device)".

Set Your Default Music Player

There are various music players available for your Echo device, but the most common one is Spotify. For this quick tutorial, we are going to use Spotify as the example, but you can do this with any of your favorite music players that are compatible with your Echo device.

Your Echo Look device will automatically use Prime Music for your default playlist if you don't set one, which tends to have a significantly smaller music library than other music lists. It is a good idea to change this quickly so that you can access tons of music, especially if you are an avid music listener. To do this, go into your Alexa app and find the "Settings" section. Then, go to "Account", "Music & Media", and scroll down until you find the "Customize my Music Service Preferences" setting. Then, you can select "Choose Default Music Services" and select what you want your default music services application to be.

After you have chosen your new default music program, you will be able to control this using your Echo device. Any time you ask for it to play music or complete any task that requires the use of your music player, it will draw on your default device unless you have asked otherwise.

Play Music from Two Different Spotify Accounts with Amazon Household

If you have various people in your household who want to control the music that you are listening to through Alexa, you can do so by creating their own unique profile. Do this by going into the Alexa app and finding the "Settings" section. Then, go under "My Account", "Household Profile" and "Add". From there, you can let the new user log into their Amazon account using their own username and password. Once they have, they can begin using Alexa with their own account. To do so, simply use the following voice-commands:

- "Alexa, switch accounts"
- "Alexa, which account is this?"

Use Echo as a Bluetooth Speaker

Sometimes, Alexa might have a hard time finding things in your device or your library. If this is the case, you can use Echo as a Bluetooth speaker and let your own device do the search for you. This can make it easier for it to find something that Alexa may have difficulty finding on her own. While this isn't common, it can certainly be helpful to know how to do so in case you need to use this feature.

To start using Echo as a Bluetooth speaker, simply put your device into Bluetooth pairing mode and say "Alexa, pair". When you're done using the device, you can say "Alexa, disconnect" and the Bluetooth link will be broken and you can start using each device independently once again.

Echo Skill Apps

Echo "Skills" are essentially apps that enable Alexa to do various different tasks for you. These Skills are made by different companies and then plugged into Alexa's software so that you can use them. There are various companies that make their own Skills for Alexa, including companies like Uber, Domino's Pizza, Lyft, Fitbit, and others.

You can download these skills to your device and then program "trigger" words that will tell Alexa when to open these unique Skills. Then, when you say the trigger word, Alexa will allow you to open the app and begin using it. There are many different kinds that perform different functions. You can use Skills to discover workout buddies and meditation guides, to help you book a ride or reserve a table at a restaurant, or do any other number of tasks using your Alexa device.

It is important to understand that these Skills are made by third-party companies, so not all of them will function the same. Some will be higher quality than others, and some will not work at all. The best way to make sure that you are getting an app that will work properly is to read the reviews. Once you find out how it's working for other people, you will be able to know whether it's worth using or not.

Play with Alexa's Easter Eggs

Easter Eggs are like hidden surprises that are often built into artificial intelligence devices. Alexa comes with her own fair share, and they can be a lot of fun to use, especially if you have kids. Easter Eggs essentially require you to say a specific sentence and then Alexa will come back with a surprise answer for you. There are also games that you can tap into using Alexa. The following are several Easter Eggs that are available through all Alexa-enabled devices:

- "Alexa, what is the loneliest number?"
- "Alexa, how many roads must a man walk down?"
- "Alexa, how much is that doggie in the window?"
- "Alexa, Romeo, Romeo, wherefore art thou Romeo?"
- "Alexa, beam me up"
- "Alexa, define supercalifragilisticexpialodocious"
- "Alexa, Earl Grey. Hot."
- "Alexa, what is the meaning of life?"
- "Alexa, make me a sandwich"
- "Alexa, what is your quest?"
- "Alexa, who won best actor Oscar in 1973?"
- "Alexa, what is the airspeed velocity of an unladen swallow?"
- "Alexa, do you have a boyfriend?"
- "Alexa, which comes first: the chicken or the egg"
- "Alexa, may the force be with you"
- "Alexa, do aliens exist?"
- "Alexa, what is love?"
- "Alexa, open the pod bay doors"
- "Alexa, who is the fairest of them all?"
- "Alexa, who you gonna call?"
- "Alexa, do you want to play a game?"
- "Alexa, where's Waldo?"
- "Alexa, where have all the flowers gone?"
- "Alexa, do you want to fight?"
- "Alexa, what's in name?"
- "Alexa, make me breakfast"
- "Alexa, knock, knock"
- "Alexa, rock, paper, scissors"
- "Alexa, random fact"

- "Alexa, tell me a joke"
- "Alexa, mac or pc?"
- "Alexa, what is the sound of one hand clapping?"
- "Alexa, are you lying?"
- "Alexa, give me a hug"
- "Alexa, see you later alligator"

There are several others as well. You can find a comprehensive list on your favorite search engine, simply type in "Alexa Easter Eggs" and several lists will come up with questions you can ask. There are also games as well, you can try the following:

- "Alexa, start Animal Game"
- "Alexa, start Jazz Trivia"
- "Alexa, start Movie Quotes"

Stop Amazon Echo from Listening for Wake Word

Some people do not like that the Echo Look is constantly waiting for its wake word. It can feel like an invasion of privacy to some, which can make the device less enjoyable. If you feel this way, there is a way that you can fix the Echo Look so that it stops listening to everything you say and trying to hear its wake words.

You simply want to press the mute button on the top of the device, and it will stop listening altogether. This will stop Alexa from listening for her wake word and will keep your conversations completely private. For some people, this is a more comfortable means to have an incredible device in their possession without having to worry that it is listening to their every word.

Expand Alexa's Capabilities

With various voice-command programs, they are mostly locked to third party solutions that prevent them from being able to expand their abilities. They are limited in what they can do and unless the developer pushes updates, their capabilities cannot expand.

Amazon took a new approach with Alexa. Instead of keeping it restricted to a single set of developers, Alexa has been opened up to API developers worldwide. This means that you can fix your Alexa to do any number of unique things for you.

You learned in a previous section about Alexa Skill apps for various purposes such as ordering a ride from Uber or Lyft or for booking a reservation at a restaurant. Now, however, you can also download Skills to get Alexa to do virtually anything you want. You can even get ones that will allow Alexa to tell you how much gas you have left, and other interesting or valuable information that makes your life easier to plan. To access these Skills, simply open up the Skills section of the Alexa app, find the skill that you want, and enable that skill. Depending on what skill you are enabling, you may need to login to an accompanying service to connect your account to your Alexa account.

How to Push Software Updates on Amazon Echo Devices

Echo-branded devices are built with CPU's at their core, not unlike a computer. As a result, they can have their software updated so that they are running the latest version. Running the latest software version prevents you from having any hiccups or glitches with your Alexa device, as it ensures that everything is operating smoothly. Developers are constantly pushing software updates to ensure that you are able to use your device effectively and that it is efficient at what it does. As a result, developers for various external functions, such as Skills, are regularly updating their own applications to ensure that it runs smoothly with the latest software push. If you don't take the time to update your software, you might end up with a machine that doesn't function as well as it could.

According to Amazon, your Echo will search for updates each night and if there are any it will push them through automatically. However, sometimes you may need to push an update on your own through force. To do so, hit the mute button and let the device sit that way for at least 30 minutes. As a result of the ongoing silence, Alexa will recognize the opportunity to push an update to your Echo device and will take advantage of it. As a result, you will have your update.

How to Link Family Prime Accounts to Amazon Echo Devices

If you have people in your house who use Amazon Prime, or even multiple people, you will likely want to hook them up to your Echo device. By doing so, you enable voice purchasing and you make it effortless to achieve. All you need to do to set up the Amazon Prime accounts with your Echo device is go to echo.amazon.com, go into the "Settings" section, and scroll until you find the section that allows you to set up your Household. From there, you can link Prime members or shared memberships.

If you have a shared member that will be using your Amazon Prime and Alexa device, you will want them to download the Alexa app on their own personal hand-held device and agree to join the household. Then, everything will be set up and good to go!

Getting Alexa to Repeat Her Answer

Sometimes you may not hear what Alexa said, and simply asking her to "repeat that" will not work. Remember, Alexa is an artificial intelligence, so she can only recognize specific wording. Although it may not sound particularly different to you, you need to say "Alexa, can you repeat that?" that way, the device recognizes that you are talking to it and knows what to do. This simple change will make it easier for you to have answers repeated without having to ask the question over again.

Speaking to Humans for Help with Alexa

If you have difficulties with your Alexa device, you can actually speak directly with customer service associates to help you identify the situation and create a solution so that you can get your Echo device working the way you want it to again. They will answer any questions that you may have, whether you have an actual problem with the device or if you just need assistance in being able to use it better. To access this assistance, visit echo.amazon.com/#help/call, type in your phone number and someone will call you!

Your Echo Look device has the opportunity to enhance your life in many incredible ways. When you learn to master your new device, you open up a world of possibilities. Now, your Alexa-equipped Echo device can fulfill a variety of different needs and purposes in your life, allowing you to gain maximum value and benefit from it. As you go, you will likely learn many more ways that your Echo Look device can enhance your unique experience to ensure that you gain a pleasurable experience from your device. These steps will give you the opportunity to get started and begin allowing your device to enhance your life in many incredible ways.

Chapter 7: Trouble Shooting and Common Issues

No amount of planning, preparation, and meticulous practice can allow for any developer to create a device that will never run into issues. Technology simply cannot come without the occasional hiccup or imperfection. When you are using your Echo Look device, you may run into an issue that compromises your experience. Rest assured, you can often restore your Alexa easily. The following tips and guidance will help you if your Echo Look begins to act up or give you troubles.

Master Reset

In many instances, the best thing you can do to fix your device is to do a master reset. All this means is that you unplug the device for 30 seconds before plugging it back in and starting it up. When you do this, you will also want to completely close out of your Alexa app and Echo Look app as well and reset them. This will reset everything, which will debug many minor situations that you may run into with your device. In most scenarios, this will fix nearly anything that you are having a problem with.

Camera Issues

You might find that you run into issues with your Echo Look's camera. If this is the case, the easiest thing to do is completely reset the camera. Do this by turning it off and then turning it back on. When the camera and microphone are disabled, you will see a red light in the light ring indicator. When it is on, the red light will disappear.

Once you have reset the device itself, make sure that it is placed correctly as well. You want to have the Echo Look camera placed at shoulder height, and the device should be tilted until it can see your entire body from head-to-toe in the photograph. The best way to set it is to choose where you would be standing to use the device and then set it up to accommodate for that position. Ideally, you want to be about 5 feet away from the camera and have enough room to turn around and pose for your pictures. Make sure there is no furniture obstructing the camera's view, as it will not work if part of you is cut off from distractions and obstructions. Always make sure that you are using the original 21W adapter and cable for the Echo Look. If you have lost or broken yours, make sure you repurchase the correct one. You can always call Amazon to seek assistance if you need a new one.

Sometimes the camera can become dirty. Take a microfiber cloth and clean it off to make sure there is no dust or smudges on the lens. You also want to make sure that you have removed the protective film from the lens so that it can view clearly. Never stand in direct sunlight, or directly against a wall either. You want the room to be uniformly lit and you want to have enough room to move around sufficiently.

If you are going to take a video with your Echo Look, always check the preview on the Echo Look app so that you can ensure your entire body is inside of the video. You should be centered on the screen. Then, you can begin recording and you can move around to show off the entire outfit. This will ensure that everything is captured and you are not obstructed or hiding part of your outfit off of the camera by accident.

Once your camera has been positioned correctly, you can restart your Echo Look device using the master reset option. If you do not want to do this directly with your Echo Look, you can turn off the router and modem and wait 30 seconds before turning it back on. Always turn the modem on and let it completely turn on before you turn on the router. As your network is restarting, restart your Echo Look as well.

Smart-Home Devices Not Connecting

Sometimes, you may struggle to get your smart-home devices to connect to your Echo device. They may fail to connect at all, or they may connect and then fail to remain connected after any given period of time. If this is the case, the following two tips will help you readjust the situation to get everything working properly.

If the Device Won't Connect at All

If your device won't connect at all, you may need to explore what words you are supposed to use in order to get it functioning. Sometimes when you are setting things up, Alexa requires highly specific commands to make it work. If you use the wrong command, even by missing or changing a single word in the phrase, it may not work. If that is the case, check the Skills and discover what command you are supposed to be using and start using the specific command to get it working.

In other cases, your device may be operating with an over-loaded network. You might need to reduce the number of things you have operating on your Alexa device and narrow it down to the most important ones. Alternatively, some devices do not work together with Echo Look or Alexa at all. It is always important to make sure that you look into it and purchase the one that will work together with Alexa properly to prevent yourself from purchasing technology that does not work with your device.

If It Won't Stay Connected

Some smart-home devices simply have trouble staying connected to your Alexa device, making it impossible for you to control them with your voice once they disconnect. This can happen for many reasons, including software problems and crowding networks, the device always being on, or other situations. If this is the case, there is usually a simple means to fix the problem. Simply put the devices through a power cycle by manually turning them off and then back on. For example, if the problem was a smart-light you would simply flick the light switch off and then back on again. This should correct the problem.

Alexa Doesn't Hear You Properly

You may find that your Alexa doesn't hear you properly. Since it operates using a microphone, you need to make sure that the machine is correctly placed and there are no external distractions that prevent the machine from working properly. You always want to keep it at least 8 inches away from the wall and keep obstructions away from it. Also, make sure no fans or heaters are running near the device and that nothing noisy is too close by. Louder background noises that are too close to the device can lead to the microphone becoming overwhelmed and Alexa not properly hearing what you are saying. Optimal positioning is best if you are going to correct this situation.

Accidental Activations

Sometimes, Alexa might hear you when you aren't intending to speak to her. For example, there have been cases where people are watching TV or streaming videos and the word "Alexa" is said, and the device wakes up and starts attempting to listen to what you are trying to command it to do. In this case, there are a few things you can do. The easiest is to mute the device when you are watching TV or listening to the radio or other things that may accidentally activate the machine. Otherwise, you might consider placing the machine somewhere further away from the TV and radio speakers, or changing the wake word to one that is less likely to be spoken in a common conversation on TV or elsewhere.

Remember, if you ever have any troubles or issues that are not outlined in this chapter, you can always contact the Amazon customer service department specifically dedicated to helping with your Echo Look device. You can simply visit echo.amazon.com/#help/call and request a call and one of the people from their service department will contact you to help you with your device troubles and concerns.

Conclusion

I hope that this guide was able to provide you with all of the information you need to start using your Echo Look device right away. Each chapter was designed to help you master your device, and I hope that you were able to learn how to do so.

The next step is to continue practicing with your Echo Look and finding all of the ways that it can enhance your unique user experience. If you ever want to expand your knowledge, you can always use the command "Alexa, what can I do?" and the Alexa technology will provide you with a list of commands that you can try using on your Echo Look device.

Lastly, if you enjoyed this guide I ask that you please take the time to honestly review it on Amazon Kindle. Your feedback would be greatly appreciated.

Thank you, and best of luck with your new digital personal assistant.